KRAKATOA

These and other titles are available in the
Lucent World Disasters Series:

KRAKATOA

by
Don Nardo

Illustrations by
Brian McGovern

LUCENT
B·O·O·K·S

WORLD DISASTERS

Library of Congress Cataloging-in-Publication Data

Nardo, Don, 1947-
    Krakatoa / by Don Nardo ; illustrations by Brian McGovern.
      p. cm. — (World disasters)
    Includes bibliographical references.
    Summary: Explores the eruption of Krakatoa in its cultural, historical, and geographic contexts and discusses the effect on both people and environment.
    ISBN 1-56006-011-5
    [1. Krakatoa (Indonesia)—Eruption, 1883. 2. Volcanoes.]
I. McGovern, Brian, ill. II. Title. III. Series.
DS647.K73N37 1990
959.8'022—dc20   90-6003
                                                                          CIP
                                                                          AC

© Copyright 1990 by Lucent Books, Inc.
Lucent Books, Inc., P.O. Box 289011, San Diego, California, 92128-9011

To Christine, who is a natural wonder
in her own right.

Table of Contents

Preface
The World Disasters Series

World disasters have always aroused human curiosity. Whenever news of tragedy spreads, we want to learn more about it. We wonder how and why the disaster happened, how people reacted, and whether we might have acted differently. To be sure, disaster evokes a wide range of responses—fear, sorrow, despair, generosity, even hope. Yet from every great disaster, one remarkable truth always seems to emerge: in spite of death, pain, and destruction, the human spirit triumphs.

History is full of disasters, arising from a variety of causes. Earthquakes, floods, volcanic eruptions, and other natural events often produce widespread destruction. Just as often, however, people accidentally bring suffering and distress on themselves and other human beings. And many disasters have sinister causes, like human greed, envy, or prejudice.

The disasters included in this series have been chosen not only for their dramatic qualities, but also for their educational value. The reader will learn about the causes and effects of the greatest disasters in history. Technical concepts and interesting anecdotes are explained and illustrated in inset boxes.

But disasters should not be viewed in isolation. To enrich the reader's understanding, these books present historical information about the time period, and interesting facts about the culture in which each disaster occurred. Finally, they teach valuable lessons about human nature. More acts of bravery, cowardice, intelligence, and foolishness are compressed into the few days of a disaster than most people experience in a lifetime.

Dramatic illustrations and evocative narrative lure the reader to distant cities and times gone by. Readers witness the awesome power of an exploding volcano, the magnitude of a violent earthquake, and the hopelessness of passengers on a mighty ship passing to its watery grave. By reliving the events, the reader will see how disaster affects the lives of real people and will gain a deeper understanding of their sorrow, their pain, their courage, and their hope.

Introduction

A Dead Island Springs to Life

During the fall and winter of 1883-1884, people around the world enjoyed magnificent, deep-red sunsets. Few were aware that the cause of these beautiful scenes was one of the greatest natural disasters in recorded history. This was a volcanic eruption on the island of Krakatoa in the East Indies, near the islands of Java and Sumatra.

In 1883, the coasts of these islands were thickly inhabited. Along the Sunda Strait, the channel of water separating Java and Sumatra, sprawled native villages, each surrounded by well-irrigated fields of rice and peanuts. Beyond the fields stretched miles of lush jungle, kept green by the region's tropical climate. Among the bamboo huts in each village stood a few larger stone dwellings, the homes of Dutch settlers. The islands were colonized by the Dutch in the 1600s, giving the settlers easy access to the prosperous trade routes of the Indian Ocean and the China seas.

Few paid much attention to the

1500 B.C.
Volcanic eruption sinks the island of Thera

A.D. 79
Mt. Vesuvius erupts, burying Pompeii, Herculaneum, and Sabiae; 16,000 die

650
Srivijaya, a small Buddhist state, rules Indonesia

C. 1000
Leif Eriksson discovers North America

1096-1219
Crusades

1492
Columbus discovers America

1519-1522
Magellan sails around the world

1590
Last Indonesian empire of Mataram establishes Islam as the primary religion

1602
The Dutch East India Company monopolizes the spice trade in Indonesia

1631
Mt. Vesuvius erupts, 4,000 die

1669
Mt. Etna in Sicily erupts; 20,000 die

1772
Mt. Papandayan on Java erupts, 3,000 die

1776
American Revolution

1792
Mt. Unzen-Dake in Japan erupts; 10,400 die

1815
Mt. Tambora on Java erupts; 12,000 die

1861-1865
American Civil War

1883
Krakatoa erupts; 36,000 people killed by tidal waves

small, uninhabited island of Krakatoa in the center of the Sunda Strait. Although native legends told of a time in the dim past when the volcano on the island had violently erupted, in 1883, everyone thought the volcano was extinct and harmless. Although some moderate earthquakes had rocked the strait between 1877 and 1880, almost no one associated the tremors with Krakatoa.

The people did not realize that deep beneath Krakatoa tremendous pressure was building. The volcano on the island was far from extinct. Huge masses of molten rock and tightly compressed gases pushed their way upward toward the dormant craters of the volcano. On August 26, 1883, Krakatoa blew up in a series of stupendous explosions that could be heard for hundreds of miles. A blanket of ash engulfed the coasts of Java and Sumatra, making day blacker than the blackest night. Fireballs fell on the decks of ships forty miles away, and heavy seas battered the villages on the coasts.

Less than twenty-four hours later, the eruption reached its peak when most of Krakatoa collapsed into the sea. Huge waves radiated outward and rushed toward the villages surrounding the strait. Within thirty minutes, more than thirty-six thousand people were dead. Meanwhile, millions of tons of fine ash spread out into the atmosphere. The ash blocked and scattered the sun's rays, creating the spectacular sunsets few would ever forget.

1902
Eruption of Mount Pelee on the West Indies island of Martinique kills 40,000 people

1939
World War II begins

1942
Japanese gain control of Indonesia

1945
Indonesian nationalists declare independence when Japan surrenders to Allies

1949
Dutch cede control of Indonesia to nationalists under Sukarno

1968
Suharto becomes president of Indonesia

1975
Indonesian Republic annexes East Timor

1980
Mt. St. Helens erupts in Washington state; 60 casualties

1984
U.S. Secretary of State George Shultz visits Indonesia because of human rights abuses in East Timor

1985
Nevado del Ruiz in Columbia erupts; 22,940 die

1989
Pope John Paul II visits East Timor hoping to halt persecution of the mostly Roman Catholic population by the Muslim Indonesian occupying forces

1990
Lava flow from Mt. Kilauea in Hawaii causes evacuation of surrounding population

One

Life on the Ring of Fire

The uninhabited island of Krakatoa is located between the much larger islands of Java and Sumatra in the Sunda Strait. These islands are now part of the modern nation of Indonesia. In fact, Indonesia is composed entirely of islands that stretch for more than 3,000 miles between the Indian and Pacific oceans. Along with Java and Sumatra, the islands of Bali, Borneo, Celebes, and thousands of smaller ones make up Indonesia's total land area of more than 735,000 square miles.

Java and Sumatra, two large islands situated in the westernmost section of Indonesia, are the closest populated areas to Krakatoa. Java is about 660 miles long, while Sumatra is a good deal larger with a length of more than 1,060 miles. Both islands lie near the equator and have a hot, tropical climate marked by heavy seasonal rains called monsoons. The abundant rain and sunlight support large jungles in the lowlands of the islands, where tigers, rhinoceros, leopards, apes, and other wild animals live. Volcanoes are common on both islands. Sumatra has 90 volcanic peaks and Java 112, more than 30 of which are active.

People have lived on Java and Sumatra for at least two thousand years. The original natives were primitive fishing people who worshipped the spirits of nature. About 700 A.D., a powerful kingdom called Mataram arose in Java. These people, who made their living by farming, had social and religious ties with the Hindu culture in India. The descendants of both of these cultures continue to populate the islands today.

Moslem traders from the Asian mainland were the first non-natives to settle the islands, in the 1400s. Many of the natives adopted Moslem customs and religious practices. Later, in the 1500s, Portuguese explorers visited the area but established few colonies. The first settlements by explorers from the Netherlands came in the early 1600s and the Dutch took an immediate liking to the islands. At first, the Dutch only traded with the natives. But soon, the Netherlands began sending large numbers of colonists.

In 1619, the Dutch forcibly took control of Java's capital, Jakarta,

singapore

SUMATRA

KRAKATOA O

jakarta

JAVA

WHERE IS KRAKATOA?

The island is located in the center of the Sunda Strait, the channel of water that flows between the much larger islands of Java and Sumatra. All three islands are part of the island nation of Indonesia, which lies directly south of the Asian countries of Vietnam, China, and the Philippines, and north of Australia. The width of the Sunda Strait ranges from fifteen to one hundred miles, and the distance from Krakatoa to the Javanese and Sumatran coasts averages thirty to fifty miles.

and renamed the town Batavia. The islands became known as the Dutch East Indies. By 1755, the Dutch had taken complete control of the native provinces in Java. In addition, the Dutch set up and controlled native rulers in many of the provinces. These rulers, along with Dutch officials, often treated the natives harshly. Those in power needed lots of slave labor to work the farms that grew large amounts of sugar, pepper, and other crops. These crops supplied the growing, very profitable Dutch trade with Europe. Natives were paid extremely poorly and had few or no rights. There were occasional native uprisings but the Dutch, with their superior weapons, always put them down.

The coasts of both islands surrounding the Sunda Strait were heavily populated with native farmers and fishermen, as well as foreign plantation owners, government officials, and traders. The population of Java in 1880 was about twenty million people, many of whom lived in the eastern section of the island near the Sunda Strait. Though the Dutch and other Europeans held most positions of power, they were greatly outnumbered by the natives. For example, an 1880 census of Bantam Province, the area of Java directly facing the strait, revealed the following population breakdown: 360 Europeans, 565,438 natives, 1,479 Chinese, and 21 Arabs. Most of these people made their living through agriculture, which was divided into two types—native and European.

The native, or smallholder, farms supplied most of the food consumed on the islands. These farms, averaging two to seven acres in size, were located alongside native villages. The farmers grew mostly rice, the mainstay of their diet, but peanuts, soybeans, and cassava were also cultivated. After harvests, the farmers sold the raw, unprocessed crops at markets in the larger towns.

By contrast, the European, or estate, farms produced commodities mainly for export to the Netherlands and other distant countries. Wealthy Dutch and Europeans supervised teams of local natives, who did the actual planting and harvesting. These plantations averaged fifteen hundred acres each and grew cash crops like sugar cane, tea, and tobacco. The processing of the crops took place on the plantations before export so that items such as sugar, tea, and quinine would be ready for immediate consumption when they reached their destinations.

The natives along the coasts of Java and Sumatra fished for their livelihoods with large, handmade nets. Nearly all catches were consumed locally by natives and Europeans alike. The bendang, a large saltwater fish, and the carplike freshwater fish inhabiting the flooded rice fields supplied most of the animal protein in native diets.

The islands had a Dutch gover-

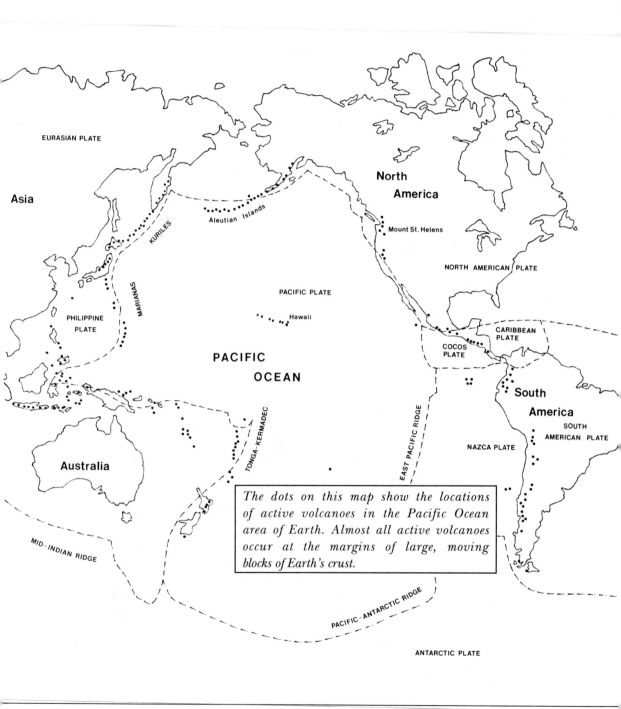

EURASIAN PLATE

North America

Asia

Aleutian Islands

KURILES

Mount St. Helens

NORTH AMERICAN PLATE

MARIANAS

PACIFIC PLATE

PHILIPPINE PLATE

Hawaii

PACIFIC OCEAN

CARIBBEAN PLATE

COCOS PLATE

South America

SOUTH AMERICAN PLATE

TONGA–KERMADEC

EAST PACIFIC RIDGE

NAZCA PLATE

Australia

The dots on this map show the locations of active volcanoes in the Pacific Ocean area of Earth. Almost all active volcanoes occur at the margins of large, moving blocks of Earth's crust.

MID–INDIAN RIDGE

PACIFIC–ANTARCTIC RIDGE

ANTARCTIC PLATE

WHAT CAUSED THE PACIFIC RING OF FIRE?

The ring of fire is a vast chain of volcanoes encircling the Pacific Ocean. Scientists call the ring the Andesite Line or Continental Margin Chain. The ring of volcanoes stretches northward from the Philippine islands, through Japan, and into Alaska. It then moves southward, rimming the coast of North America. As it penetrates the continental United States, the ring passes through the states of Oregon and Washington, and includes Mounts Hood, Jefferson, Baker, and Rainier, as well as Mount Saint Helens, which erupted in 1980. The chain of volcanoes continues southward through Mexico and South America. It then moves across the South Pacific through New Zealand and into the East Indies. There, the volcanoes of Java, Sumatra, and Krakatoa form the ring's westernmost edge.

Although not all the questions scientists have about volcanoes have been fully answered, the existence of those in the ring of fire can be partially explained by *plate tectonics*. This is the theory that the earth's outer layer, the lithosphere, is like a huge eggshell with many cracks that divide into sections. These sections are rigid, rocky plates that float on a softer, more fluid layer of hot, pliable rock called the mantle or aesthenosphere. The plates in the lithosphere continually move and either collide, slip by, or dive under one another. This movement is very slow, however, and cannot be detected for many years.

Volcanoes form on the edges of these plates in two ways: subduction zones and rifts. In subduction, one plate grinds beneath the other, creating a fissure, or crack, that sends magma (molten rock) up to the surface. In rifts, heat from beneath the earth forces surface plates apart, again creating a weak spot in which magma can be released to the surface.

The ring of fire sits on the pacific plate. If one were to take a map and place a dot for every volcano in the ring, the dots would outline the edge of the Pacific Plates.

nor-general, who administered the territory from the seat of Dutch power—Batavia (now renamed Jakarta and the capital of Indonesia)—situated in Java. Batavia was located about eighty miles inland from the eastern bank of the Sunda Strait. The governor-general had representatives, called residents, who lived in smaller towns and managed the affairs of the various provinces. All important civil posts were held by the Dutch or other Europeans. The natives who did not farm or fish usually worked as laborers on government projects or as servants in European households.

The Europeans not only controlled the economic and political affairs of the islands; they also ran the schools. Only Europeans received decent educations, although a few natives became well-educated by working as assistants to European engineers, doctors, and other professional people. The Dutch and other Europeans also lived in the best houses, buildings of brick or stone surrounded by well-kept lawns and flower gardens. By contrast, the natives lived in closely spaced rectangular dwellings with bamboo walls and palm-thatched roofs. Such houses, which could be constructed in a day or two, had been built on the islands for more than a thousand years.

The Dutch introduced to the islands, not only a European colonial system, but also the Christian religion. Although a few of the natives converted, most chose to continue following Islam, which had been the most prevalent religion in the area since the Moslems had settled there in the 1400s. There were also a few natives who clung to beliefs that had survived since ancient times. They belonged to primitive animistic cults whose members worshipped the spirits of nature. The followers of these cults claimed that Orang Aljeh, the mountain ghost, haunted the volcano on the island of Krakatoa. Sooner or later, they said, the spirit would go on the prowl and punish the Dutch for taking over the area.

Before the fateful summer of 1883, Krakatoa measured roughly five miles long by three miles wide. Three volcanic cones formed the summit of a single volcano, most of which lay submerged under the waters of the Sunda Strait. The largest of the cones was called Rakata, the others Danan and Perboewatan. Krakatoa and two rocky neighboring islands, Lang and Verlaten, were located in the middle of the strait, which, by the 1880s, had become a busy seaway between the Indian Ocean and the China seas. Rising nearly twenty-seven hundred feet above the surface of the strait, Krakatoa was plainly visible to the people living thirty to fifty miles away on the coasts of Java and Sumatra. But because of its remote location, far from populated areas, no permanent settlement was ever established on the island. A small penal colony

was built on the slopes of the volcano in 1809, but it was abandoned after only a few years of operation. Later, pirates periodically used the island as a base of operations. But, by 1883, Krakatoa was inhabited only by rodents and other small animals, which scurried through the thick green vegetation covering the volcanic slopes.

Krakatoa's volcanoes had remained dormant for years, and everyone who lived near them assumed they were extinct. Only the natives thought otherwise. According to their legends, Krakatoa had violently erupted some time in the distant past. In those days the islands of Java and Sumatra were joined together, but Krakatoa hammered them apart and remained in the strait to guard its handiwork, the natives believed. A prophecy, handed down from generation to generation, predicted that Java and Sumatra would be reunited in another great catastrophe, "when three thousand seasons have passed away." But because the disaster mentioned in the legend could not be dated, no one knew when the seasons began to be counted; there was no way to tell when the mythical rejoining of the islands might occur.

In 1883, scientists' predictions about Krakatoa were as unreliable as the prophecies of the legends. Volcanologists, scientists who specialize in the study of volcanoes, did not realize that Krakatoa lay above a weak spot in the earth's crust. They did not know that the island was part of a huge system of such weak spots, each topped by a volcano. That system is the Andesite Line. Studded with hundreds of volcanoes, the line can be traced around the perimeter of the Pacific Ocean, so it is also known as the Pacific ring of fire. No one knew that huge masses of molten rock were pushing steadily toward the surface below Krakatoa's volcanic peaks. Part of the native prophecy was about to be fulfilled. Soon, Krakatoa would erupt again.

Two

A Sleeping Giant Awakens

On the morning of May 20, 1883, Dr. Van der Stok, the director of the scientific observatory in Batavia, sat in his study reading the local newspaper. Suddenly, the doors and windows rattled, and he thought he heard artillery firing in the distance. Mrs. Van der Stok came in from the kitchen and complained that the vibrations had shattered one of her best china plates. As the windows continued to bang and rattle, the doctor became annoyed.

Van der Stok decided that the booming noises must be the sounds of an erupting volcano. He came to this conclusion because there were many active volcanoes on the islands and he was used to the sounds of eruptions. But this noise still puzzled him. It came from the west, whereas Java's largest active volcanoes were located to the south of his home in Batavia. To study the matter further Van der Stok walked to the observatory which adjoined his house.

There Van der Stok checked his instruments and noted that the rumblings could not have been earthquake tremors. Perhaps, he thought, a volcano might be erupting in Sumatra, which, like Java, had many large volcanic peaks. He did not suspect Krakatoa because the volcano there was very small and, in any case, known to be extinct. From a window in the observatory, Van der Stok could see other Dutch colonists, as well as many natives, milling about in the streets and arguing over the source of the ominous rumblings. Van der Stok concluded his observations by noting in his official diary that the noises had started at 10:55 A.M.

Eighty miles to the west, along the coast of the Sunda Strait, the rumblings were a good deal louder. In the picturesque Javanese port town of Anjer, the thundering noises shook the walls of houses. Mr. Schruit, the town's telegraph operator, focused his telescope on the strait. He could see the coastline of Sumatra about thirty miles to the west, and, beyond, the hazy outlines of that island's huge volcanic peaks. No smoke rose from the great volcanoes, so he reasoned that they were not the source of the mysterious booming.

Then Schruit pointed his scope

toward the center of the strait. He saw the familiar outline of three islands—Lang, Verlaten, and Krakatoa—about forty miles distant, and noticed a small column of steam rising from Krakatoa. But Schruit was sure that this could not be the origin of the noise. Dutch officials had confirmed many times that Krakatoa's burned-out craters were long dead. Before putting down his scope, Schruit noticed the Dutch mail ship, the *Zeeland*, making its way through the strait.

On board the *Zeeland*, Captain Mackenzie noted in his log that something strange was happening on Krakatoa. The ship had just passed within five miles of the island, and Mackenzie and his crew saw steam and debris rising from Perboewatan, the northernmost and smallest of the volcano's three craters. Sounds like artillery fire issued from the mountain and the ship's compass needle spun around erratically.

Later in the afternoon, sailors on other ships in the strait saw a large, dome-shaped cloud rise from Krakatoa and billow to an estimated height of thirty-six thousand feet. Showers of yellow ash fell on the decks of the *A.R. Thomas* and the *Elizabeth*. The captain of the *Actea*, sailing 150 miles west of the strait, wrote in his log that the eastern sky had taken on peculiar shades of green and blue. At 2:00 P.M., a dark cloud descended on the ship and visibility was reduced to one hundred yards. The captain thought at

KRAKATOA'S FIRST VOLCANIC CYCLE

Scientists have studied Krakatoa extensively since its 1883 outburst and reconstructed a picture of its first volcanic cycle. They believe that Krakatoa was born more than half a million years ago when hot gases and molten rock burst through the floor of the Sunda Strait and began building a volcanic cone. After many years, the cone grew large enough to reach the water's surface. Century after century, repeated eruptions slowly enlarged the cone until it became ten thousand to twenty thousand feet high. By that time, the base of the cone measured some twenty-five miles in circumference, and the volcano may have completely filled the strait.

The end of the cycle came perhaps ten thousand to fifty thousand years ago. At that time, the huge volcano released vast amounts of material in a short but spectacular eruption. The cone then collapsed, creating a caldera several miles wide. The sea rushed into this gaping hole, and the Sunda Strait reopened, or at least greatly widened. Primitive people living in Java may have witnessed the catastrophe, for this scenario closely matches the events described in ancient Javanese legends. These tales tell of a time when Java and Sumatra were joined together, only to be violently separated by the eruption of Krakatoa.

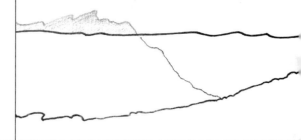

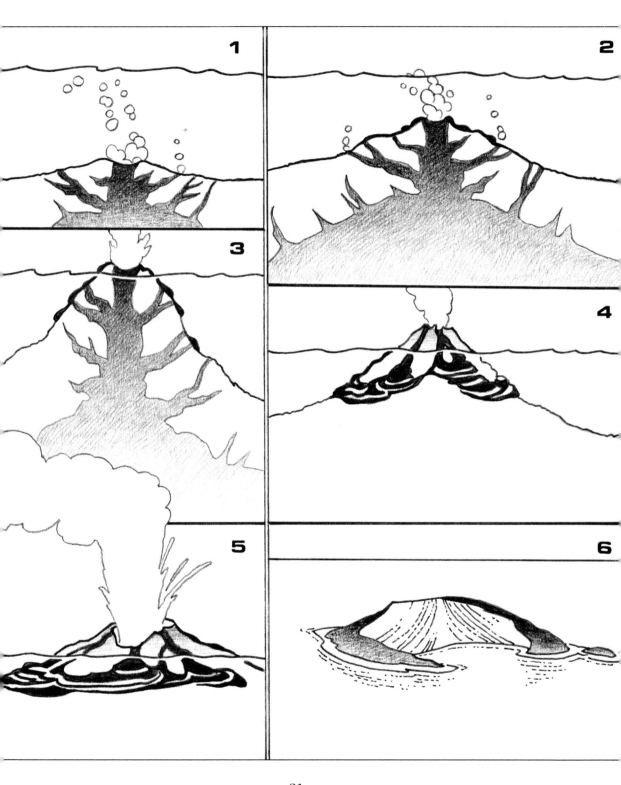

first that it was a rain cloud, but then he saw a layer of fine ash building up on the *Actea*'s decks and rigging.

About 180 miles to the northeast of the *Actea*, at Kalimbang on the coast of Sumatra, thousands of people watched the columns of steam rise above Krakatoa. Mr. Beyerinck, a Dutch official, and his wife, whose home in Kalimbang overlooked the Sunda Strait, had heard the loud booming earlier. When their native servants insisted that the sounds came from Krakatoa, Mrs. Beyerinck refused to believe it. She told them Krakatoa was extinct. The servants insisted that Atnoe Laoet, the sea ghost who lived on the island, was clearly angry. Seeing the clouds forming above Krakatoa in the afternoon, Mrs. Beyerinck started to realize the natives may have been right—the volcano did not look inactive.

The next day, Mr. Beyerinck and another official sailed a small boat to Krakatoa and saw a huge hole on the beach below Perboewatan. Fire and smoke shot out of the hole as well as from Perboewatan's crater. After returning to Kalimbang, they telegraphed Batavia and informed the authorities that Perboewatan was indeed active.

Hearing this and other similar reports during the next few days, the governor-general at Batavia ordered A.L. Schuurman, a Dutch mining engineer and scientist to investigate the eruption firsthand. Schuurman quickly gathered his tools and instruments and made his way to the docks. There, he boarded the *Gouveneur General Loudon*, commanded by Captain Lindemann. The ship sailed from Batavia in the evening of May 26. By midnight, the *Loudon* reached Anjer, and Schuurman could see a fiery glow on the horizon in the center of the strait.

Arriving at Krakatoa on the morning of May 27, Schuurman was struck by how different the island looked from his previous visits. The green vegetation was gone and the surface of the island appeared to be a wasteland. Schuurman reported,

> The southern slope was smothered with a thick layer of grey ashes from which arose an occasional withered and twisted tree . . . like naked spectres, meagre remains of the thick, impenetrable forest which had until recently covered the island. From the middle of this dark and desolate countryside . . . a powerful column of smoke . . . was hurled into the sky with the crush of thunder to a height of 3,000 feet.

As the *Loudon* sailed around the island, Schuurman saw that nearby Verlaten island was so covered with ash that it looked like a winter snow scene. Later in the morning, Schuurman and some Dutch sightseers landed a small boat on the beach below Perboewatan and went ashore. The people trudged slowly through the drifts of ash, which came up to their knees. As they climbed the side of the volcano, they saw huge bubbles rising from small boiling ponds of sulphur two hundred yards from the summit of the crater. Reaching the top of Per-

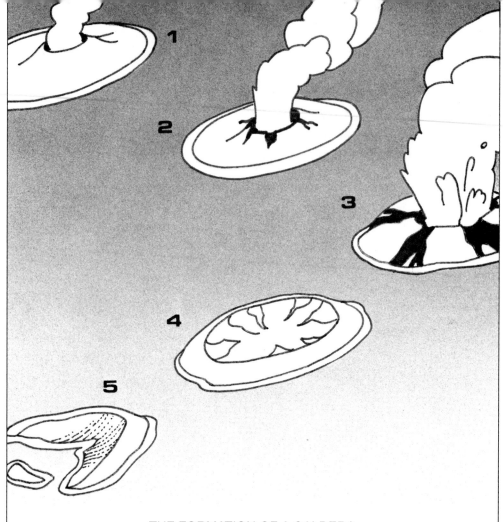

THE FORMATION OF A CALDERA

A caldera forms after a volcano has experienced many conventional eruptions. During such eruptions, the volcano releases large amounts of ash, pumice, and lava. These materials add to the mountain's size. Eventually, the volcanic cone (or cones) gets very large. Normally, rising heat currents force molten materials upward at a rate sufficient to keep the chambers within the semihollow cone filled. The outward pressure of these materials helps support the massive walls of the cone. A few volcanoes occasionally experience an unusually large eruption. In such an outburst, the volcanic materials are released very quickly in a series of gigantic explosions. The interior chambers of the volcano drain too rapidly to be replenished from below. Soon, the walls of the cone, having lost much of their support, hang above a void. Within hours, or at most days, the cone collapses of its own weight, forming a wide circular depression—a caldera.

When the collapse of a volcano occurs on land, the result is that shock waves, earth tremors, and landslides are generated. These can be dangerous to people living nearby. If a caldera forms in the sea, water rushes into the crater. The water quickly fills the depression, then rebounds and creates large waves. These waves then gather speed, and, as they reach land, height. The huge walls of water destroy everything that lies in their wake.

boewatan, Schuurman estimated the crater to be thirty-three hundred feet in diameter and nearly eight hundred feet deep.

After May 27, the eruption on Perboewatan appeared to subside and Krakatoa remained quiet for two weeks. Then, on June 16, the neighboring crater of Danan sprang to life. It erupted, much the same way Perboewatan had, through July and into August. On August 10, H.J.G. Ferenzaar, a local engineer, visited the island and noted that the surface was completely covered by a thick ash layer. He also saw that Rakata, the largest of the island's three craters, was beginning to release clouds of steam and volcanic stones of pumice, a lightweight glass.

In the days that followed, a huge black cloud hung over Krakatoa, and people on the coasts of the strait could no longer see the island's summit. The explosions and rain of ash and pumice continued. Dutch officials no longer doubted that Krakatoa was an active volcano. They hoped the eruption would end soon, for the volcano's detonations kept many people awake at night, even at distances of several hundred miles. Most people were not frightened, for they were used to the sounds of erupting volcanoes. No one knew that the eruption was far from over. In fact, the nearly three months of violent outbursts were only a tiny prelude to much more devastating events. Krakatoa was nearing the climax of

another volcanic cycle.

A volcanic cycle takes place over the course of thousands or millions of years. First, a volcanic cone slowly builds up. During this time, the volcano undergoes many conventional eruptions, expelling ash and lava, which add to the mountain's bulk. Eventually, an unusually violent eruption occurs, during which the lava-filled chambers inside the volcano empty very quickly. There is not enough time for new eruptive materials to refill the chambers from inside the earth, so the heavy walls of the volcano's cone are now unsupported. Within minutes or hours, the walls collapse of their own weight, forming a *caldera*, or huge circular crater. The formation of the caldera represents the end of the cycle. Then a period of inactivity follows, after which volcanic materials surface once more and a new cycle begins. Another volcanic cone slowly grows and fills in the caldera.

Caldera's Present Danger

Caldera formation presents a danger to people living nearby because the collapse of a volcanic cone is an extremely violent event. It produces earth tremors and landslides that can destroy whole towns. When the cone is located in the ocean, as Krakatoa was, the situation is even more dangerous. This is because water can rush into the newly formed crater, rebound out of it, and rush out in all directions. This creates large sea waves, or *tsunamis*.

ANJER IN 1883—PORTRAIT OF A JAVANESE TOWN

Anjer was the principal port town of Bantam Province, the section of Java bordering the Sunda Strait. It was very similar to many of the other port towns on the coasts of Java and Sumatra, and was the closest town to the island of Krakatoa. Anjer was built around the mouth of a large river that flowed through a nearby picturesque valley and emptied into the strait. European vessels often stopped at the town to unload supplies and pick up a guide who knew the local waters.

Newcomers to Anjer usually commented on the beauty of the town's setting. The bay was ringed by coconut palms and tropical fruit trees. Visible through the lush foilage were many white buildings with red-tiled roofs. Behind the town stretched the peaceful green valley, beyond which loomed the imposing peaks of two distant volcanic mountain ranges.

The European residents lived in stone villas surrounded by gardens. The town also had Chinese and Arab quarters, each with many wooden shops. The local natives lived in a separate village, or *campang*, within the town, in houses made of bamboo and thatch. Several other populous campangs spread out into the valley. Through Anjer ran a wide road which linked the town with others along the coast of the strait. On an average day, the road was well-traveled by people heading to and from market.

By August 26, tremendous subterranean pressures had built up beneath Krakatoa. Shortly after noon, a series of thunderous detonations sounded across the Sunda Strait. A pillar of steam and volcanic debris shot skyward from Krakatoa to a huge height—more than seventeen miles. As the explosions continued, they could be heard more than a thousand miles away. At his home in the highlands of central Java, R.D.M. Verbeek, an engineer and prominent geologist, heard the distant roar. Verbeek, who made a study of Krakatoa in 1880, realized the eruption must be reaching its peak. He telegraphed his friend, Dr. Van der Stok, at the observatory in Batavia and asked what was happening. Van der Stok replied that Krakatoa was "vomiting fire and smoke," adding that the blasts had commenced at 1:06 P.M.

Millions of people on Java and Sumatra became frightened by the noises from Krakatoa, which a visiting European called "indescribably awful." Many natives said that the spirits of nature were preparing to vent their anger on the Dutch for colonizing the islands. The Dutch laughed at the native superstitions and insisted that smoke and loud noises were the worst Krakatoa had to offer. But they were wrong. As one writer later put it, August 26, 1883, was "a date forever memorable in the long and fearful story of man's struggle with nature. Krakatoa hoisted her battle flag and gave warning that the preliminary sparring was over. The decks were cleared for action."

That day, tens of thousands of people tried to ignore the mountain's incessant roaring and get on with their daily routines. Little did they know that they had less than twenty-four hours to live.

Three

Night of the Killer Waves

During the afternoon of August 26, 1883, as Krakatoa blasted away in the Sunda Strait, a vast cloud of dark ash spread over the coasts of Java and Sumatra. In the space of an hour, the ash blotted out the face of the sun and an artificial night descended upon an area of hundreds of square miles. At Anjer, telegraph operator Schruit sent a message to Batavia warning that Krakatoa was in full eruption. He said that at 2:00 P.M. it was so dark out "that one's hand cannot be seen when held before the eyes." He added that he had gone down to the beach and noticed that the water's surface rose and fell in a strange manner.

Another resident of Anjer reported that the explosions from the volcano:

sounded louder and louder until the ground shook sensibly. The poor natives, thinking that the end of the world had come, flocked together like sheep, and made the scene more dismal with their cries and prayers. Evening set in. The detonations, far from diminishing, increased in violence, startling the people with new crises every two or three minutes.

The air on the coasts became choked with sickening sulphurous fumes. Many of Anjer's inhabitants grabbed what valuables they could and fled for the hills behind the town. In the inky darkness, they feared entering the jungles that swarmed with frightened tigers, pythons, and other beasts.

Meanwhile, Captain Lindemann of the *Loudon* docked at Anjer and picked up 111 passengers bound for Telok Betong on the Sumatran coast. About 3:00 P.M., the *Loudon* departed from Anjer, and Lindemann attempted to steer well to the east of Krakatoa.

At the same time, a British ship, the *Charles Bal*, sailed into the Sunda Strait on its way to Hong Kong. Unaware of the danger, Captain W.J. Watson headed the vessel directly toward Krakatoa. In late afternoon, the ship passed within ten miles of the erupting island. Watson noted in his log that volcanic materials were "being propelled from the north-eastern point with great velocity." Fearing that flying debris would tear the ship's sails, Watson ordered that most of the canvas be tied up. Without the sails the ship could move only very slowly. At the

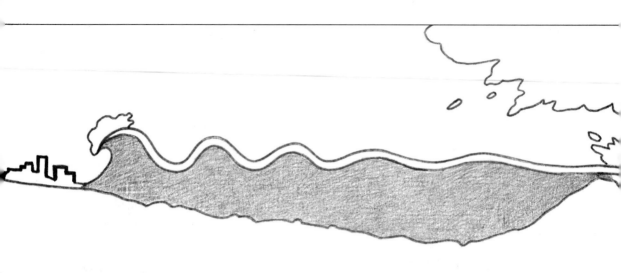

TSUNAMIS—MIGHTY WALLS OF WATER

The name tsunami comes from the Japanese words *tsu*, "harbor," and *nami*, "wave." Tsunamis are huge ocean waves that can rush ashore, destroying towns and lives. Although they are frequently referred to as tidal waves, tsunamis have nothing to do with the tides. Instead, they are caused by undersea earthquakes and landslides, volcanic eruptions, and similar *seismic*, or tremor-causing activity. For this reason, scientists also call tsunamis seismic sea waves.

When an undersea seismic event, such as an earthquake or a caldera occurs, it disturbs the surrounding water. The water is displaced and begins to move. This great mass of moving water is what makes up a tsunami. Such waves move outward in concentric circles, similar to the ripples formed by a rock thrown into a pond. The speed and size of a tsunami depend on the depth of the water. The deeper the water, the faster and higher the wave. Wave speeds of two hundred miles an hour are common, and speeds of five hundred miles an hour or more are possible.

Far out at sea, the bulk of a tsunami remains under the surface, and ships are often scarcely aware that the wave has passed beneath them. However, as the wave approaches the shore, where the water is shallow, it slows down, piles up into a giant crest, and smashes inland. Tsunamis can sometimes cause death and destruction in areas very far away from their place of origin. For instance, the 1964 "Good Friday" earthquake in Alaska produced waves that washed ashore two thousand miles away in Crescent City, California. Twelve people drowned and 150 stores were destroyed.

mercy of the choppy seas near the volcano, the vessel swayed back and forth. Then, a hail of ash and pumice stones began falling on the decks, reaching a thickness of four inches in only a few minutes. By evening, Watson saw "chains of fire" leaping toward the sky from the craters of the volcano.

A German ship, the *Berbice*, also experienced the flashes of fire and lightning produced by the clouds of ash from the volcano. Situated about twenty miles from the *Charles Bal*, the *Berbice* headed for Batavia. Captain William Logan thought at first that a tropical storm had set in and, like Captain Watson, he shortened his sails. Soon, however, a rain of ash began to fall and Logan realized a volcano was erupting nearby. Logan became worried because the ship was carrying petroleum, which catches fire easily. He ordered the crew to drop anchor in the center of the strait.

Later that night, the ash fell much more heavily on the *Berbice*, and the detonations from the volcano seemed deafening. Then, without warning, a volcanic lightning storm struck the ship. Later, Logan wrote in his log, "Lightning flashes shot past around the ship. Fireballs continually fell on the deck and burst into sparks. . . . The man at the rudder received heavy shocks. . . . The copper sheathing of the rudder became glowing hot from the electric discharges." Lightning bolts struck many other crew members, including Logan himself, who was shocked so badly he was unable to move for several minutes.

As the ships in the strait fought the ash falls and lightning storms, waves five to ten feet tall battered the nearby coasts. At Kalimbang, only twenty-four miles from the erupting volcano, Mrs. Beyerinck wanted to flee to a small house the family owned on the slope of a hill farther inland. At first her husband refused to leave, saying that the emergency was not yet great enough.

But by 8:00 P.M., the waves had begun to lap at the yard and Mr. Beyerinck decided to follow his wife's advice. They gathered up their infant son and were about to leave when one of their servants excitedly informed them that the sea was gone. "How could it have gone?" asked Mrs. Beyerinck. "Then," she described later, "I heard, above the noise of the pumice falling on the roof, above the thunder from the mountain, a frightful roaring which approached at lightning speed. My hair stood on end." A huge wave washed up on the shore and destroyed the smaller buildings near the house. Terrified that larger waves might be on the way, the Beyerincks and their servants immediately headed inland.

The waves pounded at the coast road so that they had to travel through a wide swamp. In the ash-choked darkness, they could barely see their way and held onto each other to avoid losing someone.

With each painful step, they sank in mud up to their knees. Before long, large leeches covered their legs, backs, and necks. Finally, the travelers managed to reach the Beyerinck's second house a few miles inland from Kalimbang.

As the Beyerincks struggled, the *Loudon* approached Telok Betong. Captain Lindemann saw that the pounding surf had washed away the bay jetty and smashed many of the docks and small boats along the shore. Deciding it was unsafe to approach the town, he anchored in the harbor near the Dutch gunboat *Berouw*. The *Berouw*'s captain had also anchored to wait out the eruption.

Krakatoa's Death Throes

That night, a tremendous rain of hot mud struck the *Loudon*, covering the decks, masts, and rigging. In the middle of the slimy downpour, the rigging began to glow in an eerie display of *Saint Elmo's fire*. Sometimes observed during severe electrical storms, Saint Elmo's fire occurs when electricity harmlessly discharges from metal objects, wires, and other materials directly into the air. The *Loudon* glowed all over with blue phosphorescent light. The natives on board desperately tried to snuff out the glow with their hands, believing it to be the work of evil spirits attempting to sink the ship.

As the seemingly endless night dragged on, no one on the shores of the strait could sleep. The deto-

nations grew louder by the hour. No one realized that the great blasts were the sounds of Krakatoa's interior chambers furiously belching forth their contents. At the rate of millions of tons per hour, the volcano drained itself. The inner chambers were suddenly empty and there was nothing to support the walls of the cone. The mountain's huge bulk, more than a dozen square miles of solid rock, hung precariously above a great abyss. At 4:40 A.M. on the morning of August 27, Krakatoa's final death throes began. Perboewatan and most of the northern section of the island suddenly collapsed under its own crushing weight and the sea poured into the void. After the newly formed crater had filled, the inrushing water violently rebounded and spread out in an ever-widening circle.

Thirty minutes later, Mr. Schruit stood repairing some telegraph cable on a bridge near Anjer. "I happened to look up," Schruit said

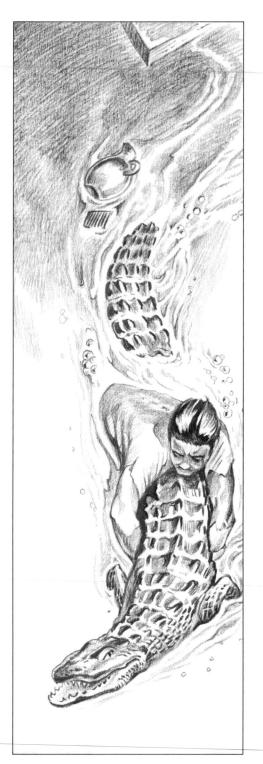

later, "and perceived an enormous wave in the distance looking like a mountain rushing onwards, followed by two others that seemed still greater." Schruit turned and ran for his life. Luckily, he managed to outrun the waves, which he and others later estimated to be at least thirty-five feet high. Schruit looked back and, to his horror, saw Anjer being engulfed by the sea. The walls of water smashed buildings, trees, animals, and people to pieces and carried the remains along in a thick, gruesome torrent. Most of the town's inhabitants died instantly.

One native survived the first wave by holding onto a tree limb. A large alligator approached and the man fought to keep the trunk of the tree between himself and the creature. Within minutes, another great wave swept the native away from the tree. Trying to keep his head above water, the man jumped on top of the alligator and rode out the current. Some time later, some friends in a canoe pulled him off the beast, which then disappeared into the floodwaters.

The waves obliterated Anjer. About the same time that the town met its watery end, the wave struck Telok Betong and other towns along the coast of Sumatra. Witnesses on board the *Loudon* saw the local lighthouse snap in two and float inland. The biggest wave lifted the *Berouw* and flung it into the town's Chinese quarter, crushing and drowning hundreds of people.

The *Loudon* also rose into the air, but the waves passed beneath it and it remained intact in the harbor.

Meanwhile, thousands of frightened natives crowded on the mountain slope below the Beyerincks' house in the hills. Some time between 5:00 and 6:00 A.M., a rain of burning pumice battered the hillside. Sheets of fire leapt across the treetops. Later in the morning, cascades of ash traveling at hurricane velocities swept in from the direction of the volcano. The ash-laden cyclones stripped the leaves off trees and smothered to death hundreds of people near the Beyer-

incks' house. Inside the house, the Beyerincks tried to keep from choking on the ash as it filtered through cracks in the walls.

At midmorning, darkness still blanketed the Sunda Strait. The inhabitants of the area had endured a long night of terror and destruction. They had no way of knowing that the worst was still to come. At 10:02 A.M., the entire central portion of Krakatoa, eleven square miles in extent, collapsed inward. From this monstrous cave-in issued the loudest sound ever recorded in human history. People heard the blast three thousand miles away, in

SAINT ELMO'S FIRE

For thousands of years, sailors have recounted tales of strange phosphorescent glows that appeared on the masts and rigging of their ships, and even around their own hands and heads. Called Saint Elmo's fire, such glows are usually harmless and have been interpreted as signs of either good or bad luck, depending on the circumstances. Saint Elmo's fire is an example of a slow electrical discharge. In contrast to fast electrical discharges, like lightning, the rarer slow varieties occur when electrical currents, present in most objects, move outward into the air. Such discharges happen most commonly during damp and stormy weather, and especially in lightning storms. Saint Elmo's fire is usually seen to flow from pointed objects, like ships' masts, radio antennas, and fingers. Often, if a person touches an object glowing with the fire, the electrical current is painlessly absorbed by the person's body and the glow disappears.

Asia, in the Philippine islands, and in central Australia. The waters of the Sunda Strait, suddenly and violently displaced, reared up into giant tsunamis and raced outward toward the unsuspecting populations on the Java and Sumatra coasts. As the waves approached the shallow water near the beaches, they crested to enormous heights, then came crashing down, pulverizing everything in their paths. They struck what was left of Anjer just after 10:30 A.M., drowning most of those who had managed to survive the preceding devastation.

At Wauran, a village one mile from Anjer, hundreds of people, frightened by the darkness and Krakatoa's detonations, crowded into an Islamic church, or mosque. But the tsunamis demolished the mosque, killing everyone inside. Nearby houses, boat sheds, and even a stone fort loaded with heavy cannon were also smashed to pieces. As the waves receded, they dragged the twisted remains of the village into the sea.

A few miles down the coast, at Merak, people looked toward the sea and saw the horizon ominously rising upward. Realizing that a great wave was sweeping in, hundreds climbed to the summit of a 135-foot hill. Moments later, they watched in horror as the wave rushed ashore, crested above them, and engulfed the hill. Of the three thousand residents of Merak, all but two died in seconds.

The waves surged over Sebesi,

north of Krakatoa, killing all three thousand inhabitants. Then they obliterated Kalimbang. At Telok Betong a huge wall of water hammered the town, crushing and drowning thousands of helpless people. The *Berouw* was picked up once again and this time hurled more than a mile inland. None of the crew survived.

In the harbor, an incoming wave raised the *Loudon* high into the air. The ship lurched violently from side to side, throwing crew and passengers against walls and ceilings, then dropped back into the harbor. Miraculously, the vessel remained right-side up and everyone on board survived. Most of the people on the coasts of the strait were not

so fortunate. By 10:45 A.M., hundreds of towns and villages had been wiped out of existence.

Along the Sumatran coast, 327 people drowned as the village of Tandjoengan disappeared beneath the deadly tsunamis. In the neighboring village of Tampang, the waves destroyed every house. Farther down the coast, at Beneawary, twenty-five hundred people died in less than two minutes. While the waves battered Sumatra, other tsunamis raced out of the Sunda Strait and headed around the northern coast of Java toward Batavia. The walls of water sped up rivers and engulfed towns lying far inland. At Tangerang, nearly seven miles from the sea, a tsunami rolled into the

town and drowned more than two thousand people. The waves ravaged dozens of other villages in northern Java.

At 11:30 A.M., the sea near Batavia started rising. Forty-five minutes later, the first big wave rushed ashore and smashed hundreds of small boats against docks and jetties. In one part of town, the water surged twelve feet above the docks and snapped the heavy chains that held the ship *Augusta* in place. An officer aboard a nearby vessel saw the water pick up the *Augusta*, along with the entire dock, and carry it toward another large ship, the *Siak*, on which many natives and Chinese had taken refuge. Said the officer:

> The floating dock with the three-master *Augusta* in it, an immovable threatening mass, loomed . . . through the haze. And suddenly . . . there came cries of fear . . . from islanders and Chinese, mostly women and children who in a panic tried to climb aboard anything that would float.

The officer watched the ships collide, causing heavy damage to the *Siak*.

Two hours after the first and largest tsunami struck Batavia, a second wave washed in, surprising the residents and causing more destruction. Afterward, another large wave followed every two hours. In all, eighteen waves pounded the town.

At 10:52 A.M. on August 27, fifty minutes after the central section of the island caved in, Krakatoa gave one final colossal blast. Danan disappeared into the great void created earlier. Krakatoa's second volcanic cycle at last came to an end. In mere minutes, the sea swallowed up the remains of the mighty craters that nature had taken so many centuries to build.

The danger to the immediate area was over, but the effects generated by the eruption had not yet abated. The clouds of ash continued to billow and expand, and the great waves still raced through the ocean. Giant airborne shock waves, set in motion by the collapsing cones, rippled outward. Even as the dazed survivors along the Sunda Strait crawled from their hiding places and began to survey the devastation, Krakatoa's ash and waves traveled outward to be felt in distant lands.

night unscathed. Lightning bolts struck the ship repeatedly and cyclonelike gusts of steam and volcanic debris pummeled the craft, nearly capsizing it. In addition, every square foot of the ship's decks, sails, and rigging was covered with a thick, cementlike mixture of ash, mud, and seawater. Many of the crew and passengers later said they considered it a miracle that everyone on board lived through the ordeal.

The *Loudon* was the first ship to travel all the way across the Sunda Strait after the eruption. From Telok Betong, Captain Lindemann at first steered a course for Anjer. But he found some parts of the strait chocked with ten-foot-thick layers of floating pumice and had to take a different route. This course took the ship near the volcano itself, and Lindemann noted in his log, "As we steamed past Krakatoa, we noticed that the middle of the island had disappeared." Several crew members estimated that only about one-quarter of the island remained intact. Rakata's cone had split down the middle, leaving behind a sheer vertical cliff almost three thousand feet high. Both Lang and Verlaten islands had increased in size due to the buildup of ash and pumice from Krakatoa.

The *Loudon* continued toward the coast of Java. Arriving there about 3:30 P.M., the crew and passengers beheld a desolate wasteland. An engineer on board the *Loudon* recorded in his diary:

Four

The Blast Heard 'Round the World

During the terrible morning of August 27, 1883, Krakatoa rained death and destruction over an area of hundreds of square miles. Even at distances of 150 miles or more from the center of the eruption, many people suffocated in hurricanes of burning pumice or drowned when huge tsunamis rushed miles inland. Yet, by a strange twist of fate, those people located the closest to the raging volcano managed to survive.

During the entire twenty-two hours of final eruption, the *Charles Bal* floated within twelve to thirty miles of Krakatoa. The great waves generated by the collapsing cones passed harmlessly through the deep water beneath the ship, and it remained upright. But the vessel did not come through the long

A horrifying spectacle presented itself to our eyes; the coasts of Java, as those of Sumatra, were entirely destroyed. Everywhere, the same grey and gloomy colour prevailed. The villages and trees had disappeared; we could not even see any ruins, for the waves had demolished and swallowed up the inhabitants, their homes, and their plantations. We had difficulty recognizing Anjer, as not one house of this lively town was left standing. This was truly a scene of the Last Judgement.

The *Loudon* anchored near the remains of Anjer and Captain Lindemann went ashore. There, he learned that most of the survivors were still in the hills. They refused to return to the coast for fear of more giant waves.

The story of the Beyerincks and the natives who took refuge with them in the hills behind Kalimbang is typical of the survivors along the coasts of the strait during the aftermath of Krakatoa's fury. Shortly after noon, about two hours after the climax of the catastrophe, the Beyerincks decided it was calm enough outside and cautiously crawled from their ash-choked house. Darkness still enshrouded the countryside. But some of the natives had torches and the Beyerincks could see the devastation on their hillside. More than three thousand natives had crowded around the Beyerincks' house earlier that morning. Now, more than one thousand of them lay dead, suffocated and horribly burned by the hurricane of ash from the volcano. Many in the area needed immediate medical attention, including Mrs. Beyerinck, whose skin hung in shreds in some places.

A native carrying a sick child approached Mrs. Beyerinck, who tried desperately to help the youngster. But a few minutes later, the child died in her arms. Then other natives warned that a forest fire ignited by the burning pumice was raging toward the hill. Already exhausted, the Beyerincks and several native companions fled toward the coast.

The Beyerincks' Ordeal

The party wandered around in the darkness, trudging through mud-filled swamps and forest littered with the trunks of trees. They were sick from thirst, but when they finally found a river, the water was thick with ash and unfit to drink. There was no food, and the bloated bodies of drowned people and animals were everywhere. Because of the darkness, it was difficult to reckon the passage of time, but Mr. Beyerinck estimated they rambled aimlessly for at least two days. All the while, the Beyerincks worried about their small son, who lay in a semiconscious state.

Then Mrs. Beyerinck saw a patch of light above. "We all held our breath," she said later, "for after such a long darkness, we yearned for God's heavenly sun or moonlight. The circle of light gradually became blood-red. The strong wind tore apart the mass of ash, and we saw the wonderful, glittering sun-

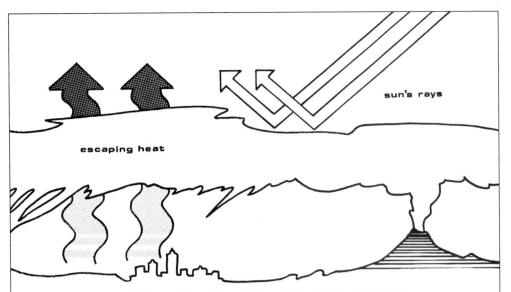

sun's rays

escaping heat

TAMBORA AND THE YEAR WITHOUT A SUMMER

Volcanologists often compare Krakatoa's 1883 eruption with an earlier eruption of Tambora. Both outbursts marked the climaxes of volcanic cycles and formed calderas. Both were located near the island of Java and both produced unusual atmospheric effects.

Tambora, thirteen thousand feet high and located on an island off the coast of Java, erupted in 1815. At the time, the Dutch East Indies were remote and relatively unknown to most Americans and Europeans. So, reports about the eruption were sketchy and the disaster went largely unnoticed by the outside world. Only after volcanologists made detailed studies of Krakatoa's 1883 collapse and compared it to other modern eruptions did the scientists go back and piece together a scenario for Tambora's mighty outburst.

Tambora's 1815 eruption may have been even greater in scope than Krakatoa's eruption sixty-eight years later. Volcanologists estimate that Tambora's explosions ejected about thirty-six cubic miles of ash and other debris before the top of the volcano's cone collapsed, forming a caldera seven miles across. Because Tambora was situated on land, there were no tsunamis, as in the case of Krakatoa. However, great heat, hurricane-force shock waves, and poisonous fumes produced by the volcano killed more than ten thousand people. Another eighty-two thousand died of starvation in the following months because the ash fall from the eruption made farming impossible.

Like Krakatoa, Tambora appears to have affected the world's weather. Scientists calculated that Tambora's 1815 eruption sent more than a million tons of ash into the upper atmosphere, where the fine particles circled the globe for more than a year at a height of twenty-five miles. This layer of ash allowed heat to escape from the lower part of the atmosphere but reflected sunlight away from the planet. This caused temperatures to drop by as much as four degrees worldwide in 1816, which became known as the year without a summer. During that coldest summer in recorded history, snow fell in New York, New England, and many sections of Europe in June. And frosts destroyed crops all over the world, leading to famines in India and other Asian countries.

light. Following the light, the party soon reached the coast, where they found the towns and villages washed away. In the distance, dark shapes floated in the sea. On closer inspection, these proved to be human and animal corpses.

Less than an hour after they reached the coast, the Beyerincks' child died. Mrs. Beyerinck was on the verge of collapse. Her hair was so choked with ash, she could barely hold her head up and she had a native shear off her tresses with a knife. The skin on her face was burned and shredded. Her clothes had been torn or burned away and she could find nothing to cover herself with. She and her husband tried to stop the bleeding from her legs by rubbing ash onto the wounds. Luckily, the next morning, some natives arrived with food. This gave the Beyerincks and their companions the strength to survive until a rescue boat arrived.

The Beyerincks learned later that the clusters of floating bodies they had seen extended across the entire Sunda Strait. This gruesome fact was confirmed by many ships, including the *Berbice*, which had been trapped and held fast by masses of thick pumice. Five days after the disaster, the ship finally broke free and headed for the nearest coast. All along the way, Captain Logan reported, the bodies of men, women, children, horses, dogs, and cats drifted in the sea. There were

also many carcasses of tigers, leopards, and other wild beasts. Apparently, the tsunamis had surged for miles into the low-lying jungles, drowning the animals. As the waves receded, they dragged the corpses out into the strait.

Logan was one of several ship captains who telegraphed descriptions of the coastal destruction to Batavia. Officials in Bantam and other devastated provinces also sent messages to the seat of government, describing the scope of the disaster. From Batavia, local news editors began sending reports to the outside world. One newspaper editor was confused by the messages he received from the provinces. He could not believe that a single volcano could wreak havoc over so wide an area, so he assumed that several volcanoes must be erupting. His story reached Byron Soames, an editor at the *Boston Globe*. Excited by the report, Soames ran to the library and hastily read everything he could find about the geology of Java and Sumatra. He then pieced together his own version of the catastrophe, in which sixteen volcanoes were still erupting on the islands. Within a few days, some other U.S. newspapers picked up Soames's story and upped the total of erupting volcanoes to twenty. Some articles reported that millions of people had been killed.

These stories did not seem exaggerated, for reports of unusual physical phenomena had come in from locations thousands of miles from the East Indies. Higher than normal tides battered many coasts throughout the world, and weather devices recorded repeated sudden drops in air pressure. Many wondered if these effects might be connected with the disaster in Java. In fact, there was a connection, for Krakatoa made its death spasms felt all over the world.

Three Types of Waves

The volcano sent out three types of waves—sound, sea, and shock. The *sound waves* generated by the great collapse traveled for unprecedented distances. Natives more than 400 miles away launched rescue boats because they thought the blasts were ship cannons firing distress signals. At Acheon, 1,073 miles away in northern Sumatra, Dutch soldiers thought their fort was under attack and took up battle positions. In Borneo, 1,235 miles from the volcano, a tribe of natives abandoned its village, fearing that the British, who had forts in the area, had launched an invasion. Krakatoa's blasts could be heard clearly 1,645 miles to the north in Saigon and 1,800 miles away in the Philippine islands. In Ceylon (now Sri Lanka), the large island located south of India and 2,000 miles northwest of the Sunda Strait, government officials ordered ships to search the local waters for the causes of the noises. And the blasts were distinctly heard on the island of Rodriguez, 3,000 miles away near the coast of

HOW VOLCANIC ASH COLORS SUNSETS

The spectacular sunrises and sunsets that occurred worldwide following Krakatoa's 1883 eruption were not the first such displays on record. Beautiful morning and evening skies were observed in Scandinavia in 1636 shortly after the eruption of Mount Heckla in Iceland. And people saw many "blood-red" suns following the 1783 eruption of Mount Asama in Japan.

Such brilliant displays result when volcanic ash thrown high into the atmosphere scatters the sun's rays. Ordinary sunlight is actually a mixture of every color. Scientists call the range of colors in sunlight, or white light, the *spectrum*. The fine ash ejected by volcanoes absorbs light, tending to soak up some colors of the spectrum more strongly than others. Blues and greens are the most readily absorbed colors. This allows other colors, most notably red and orange, to pass through the ash layer and reflect off clouds, producing beautiful visual panoramas.

Africa. Never in recorded history had people heard sounds over such great distances.

The *sea waves* that engulfed the towns and villages along the Sunda Strait spread outward into the Indian Ocean at a speed of more than three hundred miles an hour. They reached the coasts of Ceylon in just over six hours. Though they had become smaller during the long journey, the waves caused a twelve-foot rise in normal tides and claimed at least one life. The waves reached India, Africa, Australia, and even Antarctica, which lies nearly eight thousand miles from Krakatoa. Scientists in the United States recorded that the sea near San Francisco, California, rose and fell at intervals between August 27 and 30. They estimated that Krakatoa's sea waves must have crossed the Pacific ocean at almost six hundred miles an hour!

The collapse of the volcano also created a huge *shock wave*. Strong shock waves can shatter windows and even destroy entire buildings. A shock wave results when a sudden burst of energy pushes violently against the molecules in the air. Like one billiard ball hitting another, each molecule transfers the energy to the next and the wave ripples outward in an ever-widening circle. Shock waves are detected by instruments called *barographs*. In widespread locations, barographs first recorded Krakatoa's shock wave on August 27. Using information gathered by these devices, scientists pieced together the track of the wave. Scientists say it shot outward with hurricane force from the volcano. Leaving the Sunda Strait at 10:02 A.M., the wave arrived at Batavia, where Dr. Van der Stok recorded it, eight minutes later. Rushing on at a speed of more than six hundred miles an hour, it reached Sydney, Australia, in just over four hours; Tokyo, Japan, in five and one half hours; Greenwich, England, in nearly eleven hours; and New York City in fourteen and one half hours. After spanning the globe, the shock wave continued on, and scientists repeatedly detected it until it finally dissipated more than six days later. In all, the wave traveled around the earth more than seven and a half times.

Other, more gruesome remains of the volcano could be found in the ocean—both in the immediate area and thousands of miles away. The masses formed by pumice ejected by the volcano floated out to sea, forming large artificial islands. Some of these islands remained intact for months. More than three months after Krakatoa's eruption, a ship steaming through the Indian Ocean passed through a vast reef of solidified pumice. The reef was so thick that, when someone threw an iron bar over the side of the ship, the pumice held the bar in place. The people on board the ship saw broken tree trunks and mangled corpses encased in the pumice, and one passenger later wrote, "The passage of our vessel left a wake of only a few feet, which speedily closed in again. . . . It seemed exactly as if we were steam-

ing through dry land, the ship acting as a plough. . . . Other ships also saw floats of pumice embedded with human and animal corpses and, as late as September, 1884, people saw an island of pumice off the coast of South Africa, nearly five thousand miles from Krakatoa.

The pumice bore life as well as death. Insect eggs carried from the land by the receding tsunamis impregnated the pumice islands. Weeks later, many of the eggs hatched. In one episode, ships in the Indian Ocean reported seeing millions of brightly colored butterflies fluttering over the pumice, desperately searching for food. Finding none, the creatures eventually weakened and fell into the sea.

In addition to pumice, Krakatoa ejected huge amounts of volcanic ash. The Dutch geologist Verbeek estimated that 4.3 cubic miles of ash blasted upward from the volcano to heights of up to thirty-one miles. Of this, said Verbeek, about 2.8 cubic miles fell back into the Sunda Strait. The rest spread out into the atmosphere. Modern scientists say that Verbeek underestimated the amount of ash produced by Krakatoa. They calculate that more than 4 cubic miles of ash remained in the atmosphere, completely encircling the planet within a month. People in almost every country reported witnessing magnificent sunrises and sunsets, which they typically described as "splendidly green" or "fiery red." These effects occurred because Krakatoa's ash scattered the sun's rays. Sunlight is made up of all the colors of the rainbow. The ash absorbed some of the colors, allowing others to pass through the atmosphere and reflect brilliantly off clouds. Such vivid displays remained common for three years after Krakatoa's eruption.

The ash from Krakatoa also affected the world's weather. Scientists have calculated that the airborne ash blocked enough of the sun's rays to cause a lowering of average temperatures in many parts of the world between 1883 and 1886. Some weather stations reported that the amount of solar radiation received during that three-year period was 25 percent below average.

In 1883, residents of cities around the world associated the name Krakatoa with dramatic news reports and vivid sunsets. For the peo-ple of Java and Sumatra, Krakatoa had a different meaning. To them, the mountain had brought devastation and agonizing death. The final results of studies made of the disaster by Dutch and British officials revealed staggering casualties. More than thirty-six thousand people died, most of them drowned by the great waves. Animal carcasses numbered in the millions. A total of 165 towns and villages were completely destroyed, and another 132 were severely damaged. Agriculture along the Sunda Strait did not recover for several years.

Those people who escaped the disaster unhurt were thankful to have lived through one of the worst natural catastrophes in modern times. But most of them paid a high price for survival. For the hundreds of thousands who lost family members, friends, and homes, life would never be the same.

Five

Rebirth of the Destroyer

The geologist Verbeek visited Krakatoa a few months after the great eruption. He confirmed that the volcano, at least for the moment, was no longer a threat to the people living on the coasts of the Sunda Strait. After making measurements and collecting samples of ash, pumice, and rock, he made a prediction. He said that volcanic materials would continue to rise from below and one day work their way to the water's surface. New volcanic islands would eventually appear in the sea-filled caldera. These islands would grow larger until they filled the crater. Thus, Verbeek warned that Krakatoa was not dead and would one day rise again.

The following year, in May 1884, a team of French scientists arrived in the strait to study Krakatoa. First, they surveyed the coasts of Java and Sumatra and found a band of rocks and debris well inland from the beaches. The scientists found "a well-marked line, running at an elevation of from 50 to 80 feet above sea-level, indicating the limit of the terrible wave." At the site of Telok Betong, they found a large, desolate swamp, marked by pools of stagnant water. The water line left by the waves ran nearly one hundred feet above sea level. Above that line, layers of ash covered what had once been lush vegetation. Returning to the coast, the Frenchmen next visited Sebesi island, which had lost its entire population to the tsunamis. The scientists found about sixty skeletons, wearing brightly colored clothes and with hair still attached to the skulls.

Finally, the scientists visited the remains of Krakatoa. On nearby Verlaten island, there was a one hundred-foot-thick ash layer. The Frenchmen took measurements of the sea where Danan and Perboewatan collapsed and found a depth of 600 feet. When the men landed on what was left of Rakata's cone, they found it covered with ash to a depth of 260 feet. One of the scientists made what seemed an astonishing discovery: a tiny red spider spinning a web in a crevice. Life had once again found a niche on Krakatoa.

Within twenty to forty years after the great 1883 eruption, many other forms of life returned to the shattered island. Thick vegetation took

root in the rich pumice-ash soil, and many species of insects, birds, and small ground animals found homes in the growing forests. In 1886, a botanist found 34 plant species on Krakatoa. In 1896, another scientist visited the island and found that the number of different types of plants had risen to 61. He also counted 132 species of birds and insects. In 1906, botanist C.A. Backer saw trees more than twenty feet tall on the shore of the island and thick grass on the slopes of Rakata. He found 137 plant species. By 1929, scientists identified more than 300 plant species and dozens of animals, including lizards, bats, pigeons, pythons, rats, cockroaches, and alligators.

Verbeek's Theory

Verbeek made three more trips to the island after his 1883 visit—in September 1884, July 1886, and June 1887. During these visits, he put forth an important theory. Verbeek believed that the volcano's cones had disappeared as a result of collapse. He noted that the central portion of the island had once risen to a height of fourteen hundred feet. After the eruption, all that was left was a vast cavity, a caldera six hundred to nine hundred feet deep and four miles wide. He roughly calculated the total amount of ash and pumice ejected by the volcano. He found that this amount only accounted for about 5 percent of the island's original bulk. That meant that no more than 5 percent of the island could have been blown into the sky. Where had the rest of the island gone? The missing material, insisted Verbeek, had to have collapsed into the seabed.

Verbeek's opinion was immediately refuted by one of the most famous geologists of that day. Professor J.W. Judd, president of the Geological Society in England. In 1888, Judd published his own explanation of the disaster. He stated that Krakatoa had "blown its head off," pulverizing the island's rocks and sending them out into the atmosphere. For several years, many scientists accepted Judd's version of the eruption primarily because his reputation as a geologist was larger than Verbeek's.

Eventually, most scientists realized that Verbeek's explanation was the correct one. Krakatoa had collapsed in the climax of a grand cycle of caldera formation. The volcano's huge, final detonations emptied the interior chambers of the mountain too quickly to be replenished from below. The unsupported walls of the cones fell inward and the sea rushed in to fill the void.

As volcanologists continued to study the process of caldera formation, they used Krakatoa as a model. The 1883 eruption was the most recent example of the caldera-making process, so scientists were able to study the volcano and its remains while they were still fresh and unchanged by the effects of

Crater Lake in Oregon was formed by a calderan eruption.

erosion. By examining the remnants of older calderas and comparing them to Krakatoa, researchers concluded that all calderas form in the same way.

The scientists found that Krakatoa's eruption could also be used as a model to study the immediate effects of caldera formation—tsunamis, shock waves, ash falls, and so on. Since the catastrophe occurred in a heavily populated area there were many reliable witnesses who provided firsthand descriptions of the event. From these accounts, the scientists gathered much valuable information about the volcano's effects on the sea, land, atmosphere, and human population. This sort of information had been sketchy or unavailable for earlier eruptions.

In time, scientists learned that volcanic caldera formation is a recurring process that takes place in many parts of the world. They concluded that a few such events were even larger in scope than Krakatoa's outburst. They used what had been learned about Krakatoa to study many other similar eruptions.

Studies of Krakatoa also helped solve the mystery of the catastrophe that created Crater Lake in the state of Oregon. This lake is an ancient caldera that later filled up with water from rain and streams. Almost perfectly circular, the lake is some six miles in diameter and more than two thousand feet deep. According to volcanologists, a twelve thousand-foot volcanic cone once stood on the spot. They have named the vanished peak Mount Mazama. About sixty-five hundred years ago, Mount Mazama erupted, then collapsed, forming the huge crater. Scientists estimate that as much as fifteen cubic miles of the volcano's cone was engulfed in the collapse. The shock waves generated by the event probably traveled around the earth a dozen times or more.

Another caldera formation in the Americas occurred more recently when Mount Cosequina in Nicaragua erupted in 1835. Facts learned by volcanologists about Krakatoa also explained how this disaster occurred. Since Cosequina was located in a remote area, scientists knew little about the eruption until they made detailed studies of the volcano in the twentieth century. They learned that Cosequina's eruption lasted three days, during which its detonations could be heard 850 miles away on the island of Jamaica. The ashfall covered an area 1,700 miles across, and the final collapse of the cone produced a caldera one and one half miles wide. Because the eruption took place in a sparsely inhabited area, human casualties numbered only in the hundreds.

No one at all died when Mount Katmai in Alaska collapsed in 1912. Luckily, the volcano was located far from civilization. However, people knew when it was erupting because its ash fell thirteen hundred miles away in Vancouver, Canada. When volcanologists examined Katmai following its eruption, they found that, as in the case of Cosequina, the top of the volcano had collapsed. They measured Katmai's crater and found it to be more than two miles in diameter and thirty-seven hundred feet deep.

The Theran Disaster

Scientists have found what they believe to be the largest and most devastating caldera-type eruption in recorded history. They estimate the eruption was at least five times more violent than Krakatoa's 1883 blast and had more far-reaching effects on civilization than any other natural catastrophe. This disaster occurred seventy miles north of the Greek island of Crete in the eastern Mediterranean Sea on the tiny island of Thera (also called Santorini). About ten miles across, Thera's circular outline forms the rim of a huge ancient caldera. Scientists have used what they know about Krakatoa's eruption to piece together an account of the disaster that created Thera's caldera.

Scientists believe that more than thirty-five hundred years ago Crete, Thera, and many neighboring islands were the home of an advanced seafaring people called the Minoans. They had beautifully constructed five-story palaces equipped with amazingly sophisticated indoor plumbing systems. One of the main centers of the Minoan culture was Thera itself, which, at the time, was dominated by a volcanic cone several thousand feet high.

In approximately the year 1475 B.C., say scientists, the volcano on Thera exploded with stupendous force, enshrouding the eastern Mediterranean region in darkness. At the climax of the eruption, the entire central portion of the island collapsed and, as in the case of Krakatoa, the sea quickly filled the newly formed crater. Scientists have found evidence indicating that Thera's collapse generated immense tsunamis, which crested as high as three hundred feet and traveled at speeds of more than two hundred miles an hour. These waves slammed into the Minoan towns on Crete and other nearby islands, demolishing the splendid palaces and drowning great numbers of people. Thera ejected a thick ash layer that ruined local farmland. The catastrophe was so great that the Minoan civilization never recovered. Many historians believe that a twisted memory of the Theran disaster survived to become the famous legend of Atlantis, the story of an advanced civilization that sank into the sea in a single night.

Many centuries after Thera's great eruption, the still active volcano reappeared when two small volcanic islands surfaced in the center of the water-filled caldera. This was what Verbeek said would eventually happen in the Sunda Strait. Verbeek's prediction came true on December 29, 1927, when an erupting island surfaced in the very spot where the craters Danan and Perboewatan disappeared. Krakatoa's third volcanic cycle had begun.

Child of Krakatoa

Scientists named the new island Anak, or child of Krakatoa. Anak grew as minor conventional eruptions continued to occur every few months. By March 1953, Anak's cone was 330 feet tall. In 1959, a second cone formed within the crater of the first. By the 1980s, Anak Krakatoa was more than a mile long. Volcanologists say it will continue to grow until it completely fills in the caldera created by the 1883 eruption. But they estimate that the climax of this new volcanic cycle will not come for at least six hundred years. So, the inhabitants of the coasts of the strait are safe for the moment.

But what about many other people who continue to live near dormant or even active volcanoes? Of the roughly six hundred volcanoes in the world, many are surrounded by populous cities and towns. For instance, Mounts Vesuvius, Etna, and Stromboli, all in Italy, lie within areas inhabited by millions of people. Vesuvius last erupted in 1944, Stromboli in 1986, and Etna in 1988. In the United States, Mount Hood is located near Portland, Oregon, a city of nearly 400,000 people. The 13,680-foot peak Mauna Loa is one of four active volcanoes in the state of Hawaii, which has a population of more than a million people. Japan, with more than 123 million inhabitants, has fifteen active volcanoes, all of which have erupted at least once since 1960.

These and many other volcanoes around the world present a constant danger to the people living around them. This is because scientists cannot predict exactly when, or how violently, a particular volcano will erupt. Although most volcanoes do not create calderas when they erupt, scientists cannot be sure which will or will not do so.

Many people who live near volcanoes believe they are safe because the volcanoes are extinct. But volcanologists admit they cannot say with certainty that an extinct volcano is really dead. They point out that people tend to label a volcano extinct simply because it has not erupted for a very long time. Sometimes a supposedly extinct volcano suddenly springs to life. Mount Vesuvius was thought to be extinct before it erupted in 79 A.D., destroying the Roman cities of Pompeii and Herculaneum. Krakatoa, too, was said to be extinct before it brought death to thirty-six thou-sand people in 1883.

As evidenced by the birth of Anak Krakatoa, the volcano beneath the Sunda Strait still lives. Writer Rupert Furneaux likened the volcano to a demon. He said, "The raging demon has sunk back into his prison cell, deep beneath the island he has torn to pieces. It will stay down there for ten thousand years, perhaps, before it again struggles to be free."

People may never be safe from volcanoes, as long as they live near them. Scientists say the surface of the earth is constantly moving and reshaping itself. Part of this ongoing process is the creation of volcanoes, which will continue to form as heat relentlessly rises from the planet's interior. Older volcanoes will periodically erupt and extinct craters return to life, and new volcanoes will be born near human habitations. The earth is still restless and many volcanic demons lurk in the dark depths, patiently waiting for another chance to burst into the light. Sooner or later, they will surface and claim more victims.

Glossary

animism   the belief that inanimate, natural objects, like rocks and trees, have spirits or souls.

barograph   a type of barometer, a scientific device that measures air pressure.

bendang   a large, saltwater fish common to the Indian Ocean.

caldera   a large crater formed by the collapse of a volcanic cone.

campang   a native village in Java.

crust   the outermost layer of the earth, mostly composed of lightweight rocks.

mantle   the layer of the earth that lies immediately below the crust. The mantle is composed of heavier rocks and is hotter than the crust.

monsoon   a heavy, seasonal pattern of rainfall in tropical regions.

plate margin   the boundary where an ocean plate meets a continental plate. The ocean plate folds under the other, creating great heat and spawning volcanoes.

pressure wave   or shock wave, a blast of energy that moves through the air.

pumice   a porous, lightweight volcanic rock.

seismic   having to do with activity in the earth's crust, such as earthquakes and volcanic eruptions, that produces measurable tremors.

spectrum   the range of colors, from red to violet, that makes up white light.

tsunami   or seismic sea wave, sometimes called a "tidal wave," a large, destructive wave.

volcanic cycle   the chain of events that leads to the creation of a caldera, beginning with the birth of a volcano and ending with the collapse of its cone.

volcanic lightning   large discharges of electricity that accompany most volcanic eruptions.

volcano a mountain formed when ash, pumice, lava, and hot gases rise to the earth's surface through a hole in the crust.

volcanologist a scientist who studies volcanoes.

Suggestions for Further Reading

Disaster! When Nature Strikes Back. New York: Bantam Books, 1978. General discussion of volcanism, with a special focus on the eruptions of Krakatoa, Thera, and Vesuvius.

Rupert Furneaux, *Krakatoa.* Englewood Cliffs, New Jersey: Prentice Hall, 1964. Best and most detailed study of the volcano and its 1883 eruption.

James W. Mavor Jr., *Voyage to Atlantis.* New York: G.P. Putnam's Sons, 1969. Excellent study of Thera's eruption and its connection with the Atlantis legend and other myths.

Staffs of the *Daily News* and *Journal American, Volcano: The Eruption of Mount St. Helens.* Longview, Washington: Longview Publishing Co., 1980. Exciting account of the volcano's 1980 outburst, with an emphasis on personal stories.

Kaari Ward, editor, *Great Disasters: Dramatic Stories of Nature's Awesome Powers.* Pleasantville, New York: Reader's Digest Association, 1989. Good overview of the eruptions of Krakatoa, Thera, Tambora, Vesuvius, Etna and St. Helens.

Index

Picture Credits

About the Author and Illustrator

The Author, Don Nardo, is a professional free-lance writer. He has also worked before or behind the camera in twenty films. Several of his musical compositions, including a young person's version of H.G. Wells's *The War of the Worlds,* have been played by regional orchestras. Mr. Nardo's writing credits include short stories, articles, textbooks, screenplays, and several teleplays, including an episode of ABC's "Spenser: For Hire." In addition, his screenplay *The Bet* won an award from the Massachusetts Artists Foundation. Mr. Nardo lives with his wife and son on Cape Cod, Massachusetts.

The Illustrator, Brian McGovern, 35, has been active in both fine art and commercial illustration for twenty years. His recent clients include AT&T, DuPont, Harvey's Lake Tahoe, and Chase Manhattan Bank. He has exhibited paintings in San Francisco and New York and was recently a published winner in *American Artists Magazine* in the "Preserving Our National Wilderness" competition. He has won several Best of Show awards in the fantasy art field and the 1987 Distinguished Leadership Award from American Biographical Institute in North Carolina.